SONGS OF THE INCARNATION

D1806355

**A collection of 24 songs in a
variety of styles, based on the
life and teaching of Jesus.**

**Words and Music by John L. Bell.
(Unless otherwise indicated)**

Illustrations by Graham Maule.

Published by the Iona Community

SONGS OF THE INCARNATION

He was in the world, and though the world
was made through him, the world did not
recognise him.   JOHN 1 v.10

This book is dedicated to George MacLeod
who has brought 'Glory to God in the High St.'

First Published 1984

Other Publications of the Iona Community

The Iona Community Worship Book
ISBN 0 9501351 9 4

Through Wood and Nails
A Record and Cassette No. 146/REC/S
which includes many of the Songs printed in
this book and was recorded in Iona Abbey.

ISBN 0 9501351 8 6
Made and printed in Great Britain by
Purnell and Sons (Book Production) Limited
Member of the BPCC Group, Paulton, Bristol

SONGS OF THE INCARNATION

INDEX

Denotes a song with full piano accompaniment. The others, with a few exceptions, have guitar chords.

Graham Maule and John Bell presently live and work in Glasgow, sharing responsibility for the Youth Work Initiations of the Iona Community. One of the central aspects of their work has been an attempt to develop patterns of worship which speak to and for people to whom the traditional worship of the church fails to communicate.

The Iona Community is an ecumenical body with over 170 members and 800 associate members, drawn from all walks of life, who share a committment to prayer, healing, peacemaking and the sharing of time and money.

Founded in 1938 by George MacLeod (Lord MacLeod of Fuinary), the Community has a residential centre at Iona Abbey and two Youth Centres on Iona and Mull. Groups and individuals are welcome all the year round. On the mainland, the Community has a peace centre in Glasgow, publishes a quarterly newspaper 'The Coracle', supports a ministry to the unemployed and a network of community or 'Columban' houses aiding the work of churches in disadvantaged areas.

Further information regarding the programmes of the residential centres may be had from The Abbey, Iona, Argyll PA76 6SN. Telephone: (06817) 314.

Further information regarding the life and work of the Community may be had from the Iona Community, Pearce Institute, Govan, Glasgow G51 3UT. Telephone: (041) 445-4561.

SONGS OF THE INCARNATION

Introduction

This collection of songs and drawings comes in response to demand and inspiration.

The demand is that of many in the church who look for music which is accessible, words that have fresh images and songs which can be used with all ages. The inspiration comes from places like the Abbey on Iona and the forgotten neighbourhoods of Glasgow in both of which Jesus lives and summons.

All the songs have been used with groups of teenagers and with congregations of mixed ages. There is a kind of religious and a kind of pop music which might be called 'performance'. This is deliberately 'participative'.

Because few song books offer advice for their use, may we make a few comments:

1) Taking five minutes before worship or a gathering where the songs will be used to teach new tunes, is infinitely preferable to asking the musicians to play them over the minute before they are to be sung. It is also of great advantage if the person introducing the songs uses his or her voice (and hands!) taking them line by line.

2) There is no need for everyone to sing everything. Some songs, e.g. the Contemporary Reproaches and Sing Hey for the Carpenter, are best sung when the verses are taken by one voice and the others respond in the chorus. This is actually more participative than having everyone do everything.

3) Having no piano or guitar is no excuse for not singing. The majority of these songs, and certainly all those to folk tune melodies, have been sung unaccompanied.

4) Successful participation depends almost 75% on the enthusiasm of the leader and the belief he or she has that others can sing. The apologetic introduction of 'a new song we'll have to learn' is as helpful as a hangman's noose.

5) The drawings are as integral as the words and may be used as aids to meditation.

These songs and illustrations are copyright The Iona Community. Proceeds from the sale of this book will go towards the development of initiatives in youth work and worship, two concerns at the heart of the Community.

John L. Bell
Graham A. Maule

Iona & Glasgow July 1984

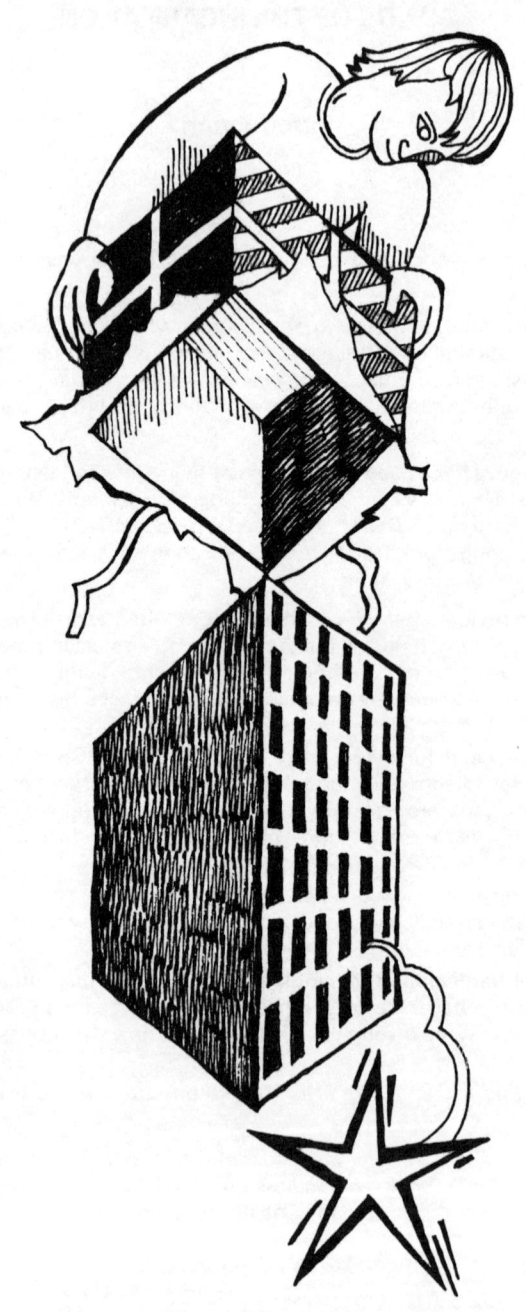

A DIFFERENT SONG

1. Sing a different song now Christmas is here,
   Sing a song of people knowing God's near:
   The Messiah is born in the face of our scorn,
   Sing a different song to welcome and warn!

2. Shout a different shout now Christmas is here,
   Shout a shout of joy and genuine cheer:
   Fill the earth and the sky with the news from on high,
   Shout a different shout that all may come by.

3. Love a different love now Christmas is here,
   Love without condition, love without leer:
   With the humble and poor, with the shy and unsure,
   Love a different love. Let Christ be the cure!

4. Dance a different dance now Christmas is here,
   Dance a dance of war on suffering and fear:
   Peace and justice are one and their prince is this son,
   Dance a different dance. God's reign has begun!

Presto

THE 'AYE' CAROL

1. Who is the baby an hour or two old
   Looked for by shepherds far strayed from their fold,
   Lost in the world though more precious than gold?
   This is God with us in Jesus.

2. Who is the woman with child at her breast,
   Giving her milk to earth's heavenly guest,
   Telling her mind to be calm and at rest?
   Mary, the mother of Jesus.

3. Who is the man who looks on at the door,
   Welcoming strangers, some rich but most poor,
   Scanning the world as if somehow unsure?
   Joseph, the father of Jesus.

4. Who are the people come in from the street,
   Some to bring presents and some just to meet,
   Joining their song to what angels repeat?
   These are the new friends of Jesus.

5. Will you come with me, even though I feel shy,
   Come to his cradle and come to his cry,
   Give him your nod or your 'yes' or your 'aye',
   Give what you can give to Jesus?

                    Come,
                    Give him your 'aye'.

1. Once in Judah's least known city
   Stood a boarding house with back-door shed,
   Where an almost single-parent mother
   Tried to find her new-born son a bed.
   Mary's mum and dad went wild
   When they heard their daughter had a child.

2. He brought into earth a sense of heaven,
   Lord of none and yet the Lord of all;
   And his shelter always was unstable
   For his mission was beyond recall.
   With the poor, with those least holy,
   Christ the King was pleased to live so lowly.

3. Can he be our youth and childhood's pattern
   When we know not how he daily grew?
   Was he always little, weak and helpless,
   Did he share our joys and problems too?
   In our laughter, fun and daftness
   Does the Lord of love suspect our gladness?

4. Not in that uncharted stable
   With the village gossips standing by,
   But in heaven we shall see him —
   Which may not be up above the sky —
   If, in love for friend and stranger,
   We embrace the contents of the manger.

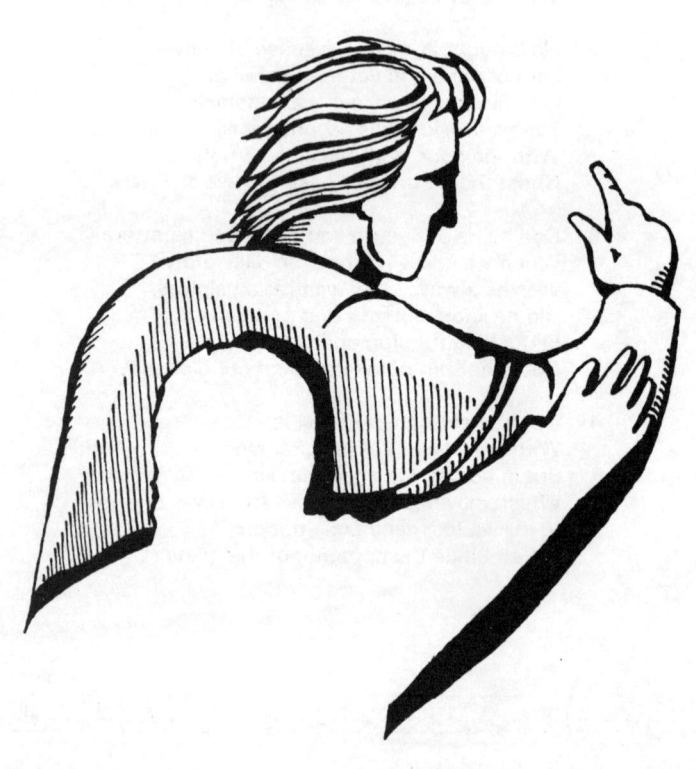

GOD ON EARTH

1. When God Almighty came to earth
   He took the pain of Jesus' birth,
   He took the flight of refugee
   And whispered 'Humbly follow me.'

2. When God Almighty went to work
   Carpenter's sweat he didn't shirk,
   Profit and loss he didn't flee
   And whispered 'Humbly follow me.'

3. When God Almighty walked the street
   The critic's curse he had to meet,
   The cynic's smile he had to see
   And whispered 'Humbly follow me.'

4. When God Almighty met the folk
   Of peace and truth he boldly spoke
   To set the slave and tyrant free,
   And whispered 'Humbly follow me.'

5. When God Almighty took his place
   To save the sometimes human race,
   He took it boldly on a tree
   And whispered 'Humbly follow me.'

6. When God Almighty comes again,
   He'll meet us incognito as then,
   And though no words may voice his plea
   He'll whisper 'Are you following me?'

WATER INTO WINE

5

Chorus: *Water into wine —*
Christ at the party makes a sign:
Water into wine —
Come, taste the best
Come, touch the vine.

Happy the wedding
And happy the blushing groom and bride.
Who will delight them
When dancing and food are set aside?

Lives full of pleasure
Are lives which are full of love and care.
When human treasure
Is spent, more is sent to give and share.

2. Laughter comes quickly
   And quickly is over, gone and past.
   Christ's joys spring deeper
   And deep joys were meant to live and last.

4. When in dark moments
   We feel that our love is running dry,
   Christ is at hand with
   Resources to trust and then to try.

Moderato

SING HEY FOR THE CARPENTER

1. Come with me, Come wander, come welcome the world
   Where strangers might smile or where stones may be hurled;
   Come leave what you cling to, lay down what you clutch
   And find, with hands empty, that hearts can hold much.

Chorus: *Sing hey for the Carpenter leaving his tools,*
Sing hey for the Pharisees leaving their rules,
Sing hey for the fishermen leaving their nets
Sing hey for the people who leave their regrets.

2. Come walk in my company, come sleep by my side,
   Come savour a lifestyle with nothing to hide;
   Come sit at my table and eat with my friends
   Discovering that love which the world never ends.

3. Come share in my laughter, come close to my fears,
   Come find yourself washed with the kiss of my tears;
   Come stand close at hand while I suffer and die
   And find in three days how I never will lie.

4. Come leave your possessions, come share out your treasure,
   Come give and receive without method or measure,
   Come loose every bond that's resisting the Spirit
   Enabling the earth to be yours to inherit.

N.B. This song is best sung unaccompanied throughout.

Blessed are the poor, who know their need
Whose lives are saved from senseless greed;
Blessed are the sad and those who cry
Who don't pretend that flesh can't die.

Blessed are the quiet in work and word
Whose lives attest they love the Lord;
Blessed are the ones whose chief desires
Lead them to live as God requires.

Blessed are the hurt who still forgive,
In whose thoughts truth and mercy live;
Blessed are the pure in heart and mind
Who turn to good the folk they find.

Blessed are all those who work for peace
Known both as doves and wild geese;*
Blessed are all those who, picked upon,
Refuse to leave God's wanted son.

Blessed is the King, who rich in grace,
Amongst the poor has made his place;
Blessed is the King who's seen to weep
Though from the grave he'll dance and leap.

Blessed is the King whose promise says
That gentle strength secures our days;
Blessed is the King who shall fulfil
The hopes of those who share his will.

Blessed is the King whose pardon sings
Through every soul which pardon brings;
Blessed is the King who lets his face
Be seen to those who run his race.

Blessed is the King who stamps out war,
Who says 'Justice is what I'm for';
Blessed is the King who gives his all
To those who hear and heed his call.

reference to the two Celtic symbols for the Holy Spirit.

The first half of each verse should be read, chorally, in time to the music. The second half is then sung.

THE SON OF MARY

1. When the Son of Mary
   Walked beside the sea,
   Nets were needing mending,
   Folk were needing free.

   Chorus: *Bless the son of Mary,*
   Bless the God above,
   Bless the Holy Spirit,
   Trinity of Love.

2. When the Son of Mary
   Walked along the street,
   Health he brought to lepers,
   Cripples to their feet.

3. When the Son of Mary
   Walked across the square,
   Children turned to dancing,
   Adults turned to stare.

4. When the Son of Mary
   Walked upon the hill,
   Mouths he fed with fishes,
   Minds with God's good will.

5. When the Son of Mary
   Walked up to the cross,
   God saw him as winner,
   Man saw him as loss.

6. When the Son of Mary
   Walked out from the grave,
   Fear was what some offered,
   Faith was what he gave.

7. When the Son of Mary
   Walks the world today,
   It's our feet he uses
   When his words we say.

N.B. This song should be sung unaccompanied throughout.

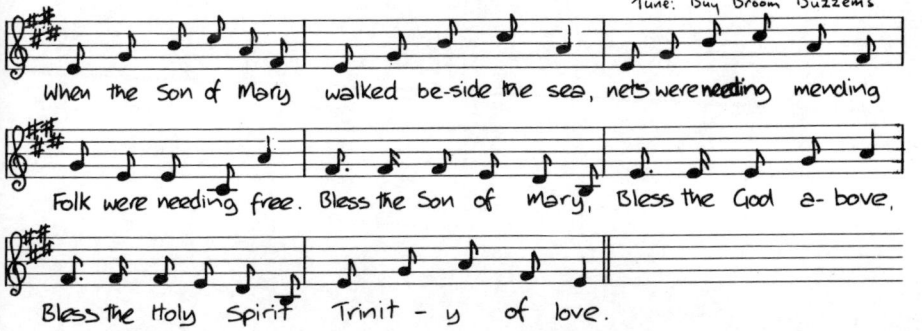

THE SONG OF THE CROWD

1. To him who walks among the crowds
   Let's show our gratitude:
   We came to him a hungry mob
   And his response was food.
   This is the teacher well renowned
   For talk of sin forgiven.
   Some prize his smile, some pull his robe,
   Some say he comes from heaven.

2. Who are you, lean-faced traveller
   Whose words surpass all law,
   Whose past was spent in industry
   With hammer, nails and saw?
   Who are you, time-served carpenter
   Now that you've changed your trade
   To hosting ad hoc lakeside feasts
   With food you never made.

3. But why the silent modesty,
   And why the shaking head?
   You're worth a thousand bakers
   For you multiply the bread!
   We'll make you king and gladly sing
   Your praise and tell your story.
   So why not stay? Why move away?
   Do you refuse our glory?

4. There goes the man whose eyes can scan
   A crowd and tell their need.
   There goes the one whose words we shun
   When keen to frown or feed.
   He walks from here while people peer
   At his all knowing face
   Which speaks of how each one who stares
   Has, in his heart, a place.

Tune: Kingsfold

THE WORD OF LIFE

1. In a byre near Bethlehem
   Passed by many a wand'ring stranger,
   The most precious Word of Life
   Was heard gurgling in a manger
   For the good of us all.

   Chorus: And he's here when we call him,
   Bringing health, love and laughter
   To life now and ever after
   For the good of us all.

2. By the Galilean Lake
   Where the people flocked for teaching,
   The most precious Word of Life
   Fed their mouths as well as preaching
   For the good of us all.

3. In the lanes of Palestine
   Where the sick sat, tired and shoddy,
   The most precious Word of Life
   Spoke the truth which mends the body
   For the good of us all.

4. Busy was Jerusalem,
   And, while critics raised their voices,
   The most precious Word of Life
   Made it clear what were the choices
   For the good of us all.

5. Quiet was Gethsemane,
   Camouflaging priest and soldier:
   The most precious Word of Life
   Took the world's weight on his shoulder
   For the good of us all.

6. On the hill of Calvary,
   Place to end all hope of living,
   The most precious Word of Life
   Breathed his last and died, forgiving,
   For the good of us all.

7. In a garden, just at dawn,
   Near the grave of human violence
   The most Precious Word of Life
   Cleared his throat and ended silence
   For the good of us all.

JESUS IS LORD

Jesus is Lord of all,
Monarch of mountain and wave,
Fuser of wind and fire,
Sculptor of crag and cave.
Jesus is Lord!
God's mighty Word creates:
Each feature worn or wild
To his intent relates.

3. Jesus is heaven's high priest;
Earth is his altar below.
Sectarian pride he chides
That Christian faith may grow.
Jesus is Lord!
God's mighty Word unites.
Those whom the past divides
He to his feast invites.

Jesus is Prince of Peace:
Atom and neutron must cower.
Hate roots their suspect strength,
But suffering love's his power.
Jesus is Lord!
God's mighty Word converts
Weapons to welcome signs
As foe to friend reverts.

2. Jesus is King of Love.
Enemy, neighbour and friend —
They, with the self, are bound
In love which knows no end.
Jesus is Lord!
God's mighty Word engraves,
Bold on the cross, that
Christ-like love disturbs and saves.

5. Jesus is Lord of Life!
To him let every mind bend;
For him let every pulse
And nerve their purpose spend.
Jesus is Lord!
God's mighty Word requires
Hands, heart and head
To demonstrate what he inspires.

GRAFT US TOGETHER

1. Christ of the black man,
   Christ of the white,
   Christ of the wronged one,
   Christ of the right:

Chorus: *Graft us together,*
Keeping as one
All that You've started,
All You've begun.

2. Christ who in strange ways
   Visits the earth:
   Here through a handshake,
   There in wild mirth:

3. Christ who brings justice
   To the oppressed;
   Christ who disturbs us
   Until we're blessed.

4. Christ of the deep truth
   Shared from the soul;
   Christ in the friend's touch
   Making us whole:

5. Christ of the traveller
   Aiming for home:
   Christ of the waver
   Blessing the gone:

6. Christ of tomorrow
   Who'll reunite
   All who today
   Move out of our sight.

Moderato

THE LORD OF ALL

The Bread of Life, the Carpenter's own son,
Has made a feast and called us to his table.
His food is simple and his words are plain
His guests need neither status, rank nor label.

Chorus: *He is the Lord of all that is*
And all that is to be,
And of me.
So let your hands meet mine
And share the bread and wine
That sets us free

He is the Alpha and the Omega,
The King of Love and thus the Prince of Peace.
What he begins shall never need an end,
The life he gives is never meant to cease.

3. He is the Servant suffering for our wrong
And yet the Lord who dances on the grave;
He helps the weak assist the very strong
And gives the poor the dignity they crave.

Each beating heart, each body and each mind
Are summoned still to answer to his call;
Whoever yearns for something greater yet
Shall find in Christ the answer and the all.

Last chorus repeat *That sets us free*

Animato

GOD'S TABLE

Since the world was young, there's a song that's been sung
Of a promise coming true;
Hungry folk will eat and long lost friends will meet
And the Lord will make all things new.

Chorus:
God has a table
Where He calls His friends
To a feast that never ends.
God has a table
And one day we'll meet Him
there.

Jesus saw a crowd that was hungry and vowed
That they didn't have much food.
So he fed that bunch with a little boy's lunch
As a sign that God was good.

3. Each and every day since our Lord went away
   To his father's table in heaven,
   Hungry people pray that, in Jesus's own way,
   We'll all share what God has given.

Taking bread and wine, Jesus once made a sign
Of the life and love that last,
And he promised then that we'd all meet again
When our time on earth is past.

5. Everybody cries, when our loved ones die
   And the parting's very sore.
   But they've found a place at the banquet of grace
   Where they'll live for evermore.

Till we hear the word from the mouth of the Lord
Saying 'Join me at my table.'
For the world we'll care and all good things we will share
As long as we are able.

1. The time was early evening,
   The place a room upstairs;
   The guests were the disciples
   Few in numbers and few in prayers.

   Chorus: Oh the food comes from the baker,
   The drink comes from the vine,
   The words come from the Saviour
   'I will meet you in bread and wine.'

2. The Company of Jesus
   Had met to share a meal,
   But he who made them welcome
   Had much more to reveal.

3. 'The bread and body broken,
   The wine and blood outpoured,
   The cross and kitchen table
   Are one by my sign and word.'

4. On both sides of the table,
   On both sides of the grave
   The Lord joins those who love him
   Their lives both to share and save.

5. Lord Jesus, now among us,
   Confirm our faith's intent
   As with your words and actions
   We prepare for this sacrament.

HE COMES

He comes, in the gathering gloom,
The man to the dark upstairs room.
He meets with his friends and he breaks
Bread he takes.

He comes, at the close of the day,
The stranger who's going our way.
He joins us at table for food:
He is good.

He comes, at the end of all time
To call, to his banquet sublime,
The faithful both living and dead . . .
As he said.

Chorus: So praise the Lord for word and sign
That at his feast we're called to dine,
And praise the Lord for bread and wine
Through which he says 'You all are mine.'

3. He comes, to stand outside our door,
The king of the rich and the poor.
He waits to be shown to his seat
And to eat.

5. He comes, as the host and the guest;
He comes, in the bread that is blest;
He comes, in the wine which is new
Just for you.
(*NO* Chorus after verse 5)

Jesus, Son of God and, stranger,
Son of Mary, born in danger,
Longed-for child in random manger:
Glory be to God on high!

2. Jesus, donkey-carried treasure,
Palm-waved prince, the people's pleasure
Pounds to heaven in mangled measure:
Let hosannas fill the sky.

Jesus, temple trade upsetter,
Gilt-edged greed needs every debtor;
Rescue faith from human fetter:
Turn the tables, let love fly.

4. Jesus, street and country walker,
Galilean lakeside talker,
Bait for cynic, sneak and mocker:
Speak the truth, unearth the lie.

Jesus, friend of saint and sinner,
Winner's loss and loser's winner,
Bread of life and host of dinner:
On your food let us rely.

6. Jesus, shame-faced Peter's brother,
Mocked by soldiers, mourned by mother,
Pilate's crowd must choose another:
Free Barabbas! is their cry.

Jesus, man of God neglected,
Jesus, God in man rejected,
Crucified and unprotected:
'It is finished!' shout and die.

8. Lord, in mercy, pardon send me;
Lord, from my worst self defend me;
By your broken body mend me.
Hear my prayer and here am I.

I walked through the lonely streets,
And I sat with the faceless ones,
And made friends with forgotten folk
But you never saw me.

*Response: Oh Lord, Oh what have we done,
For we never find you among us?*

I stood close to your window-pane,
And I knocked on your tight-shut door,
But so full and busy is life
Who am I to disturb you?

3.   I gave you a hammer and nails
     And wood from a living tree,
     And, just for the carpenter's son,
     What a present you made for me.

To those whose eyes were blind
I gave light so that they could see,
But what can I do for you
Whose look is seldom for me?

N.B. This song is best sung using a cantor or soloist who sing the verses at speech rhythm, with the response being sung by all, at first angrily.

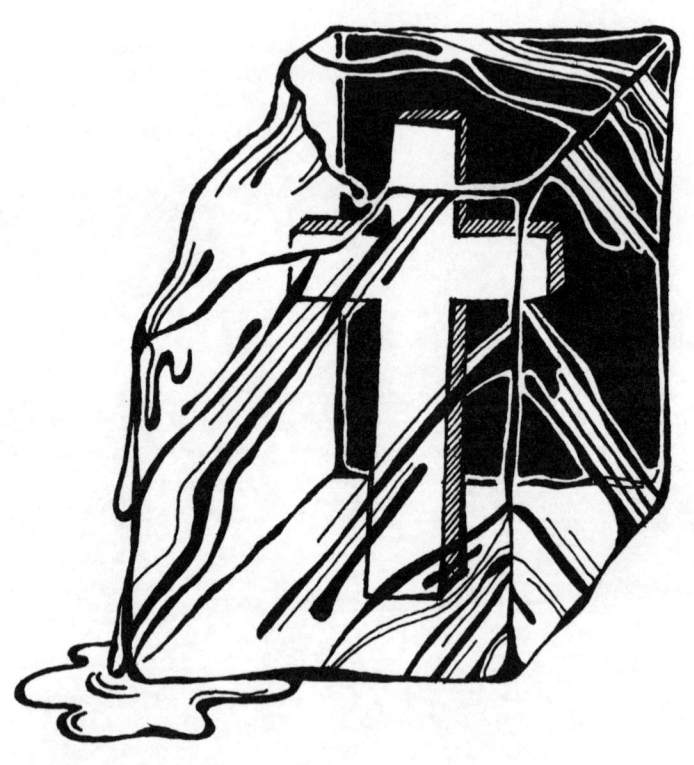

1.   Lord Jesus Christ, shall I stand still
And stare at you hung on the tree;
Or shall I move to where you move
And die and live again for me?

2.   Shall I to sin and failure cling
Consorting with the guilt I hate;
Or shall I on your shoulders fling
The wrong I breed and contemplate?

3.   Shall I your story read and tell
To note your mark on history;
Or shall I make your story mine
And live by faith and mystery?

4.   Shall I embrace the love you show
And covet this sweet holy thing;
Or of that love shall my heart speak,
My hands relate and my voice sing?

5.   Shall I retreat from where you fall
And seek a safer path through life?
Or shall I join you in the world
Where peace is scarce, injustice rife?

6.   Lord Jesus Christ, the God who lives
To love and die and rise again,
Make me the who, and you the why,
Your way the how, and now the when.

Tune: Rockingham

Lord Je-sus Christ, shall I stand still and
stare at you hung on the tree or
shall I move to where you move and
die and live a-gain for me.

RESURRECTION MORNING

1. Cantor: See how a light shines from the tomb
    Response: *Oh come and tell us more*
    Cantor: Jesus has left his second womb
    Response: *Oh come and tell us more.*

    Chorus: *ALLELUIA, ALLELUIA,*
                                                ALLELUIA, ALLELUIA.

2. A gardener sees a woman sad
    Then says he's Christ and makes her glad.

3. Those for whom faith is almost dead
    He fills with life and love instead.

4. The powerful ones who live by might
    Are freed by Christ to live by light

5. See where disciples are afraid,
    He shows the marks the nails have made.

6. The light of Christ shines on our way
    Back from the grave he's here to stay.

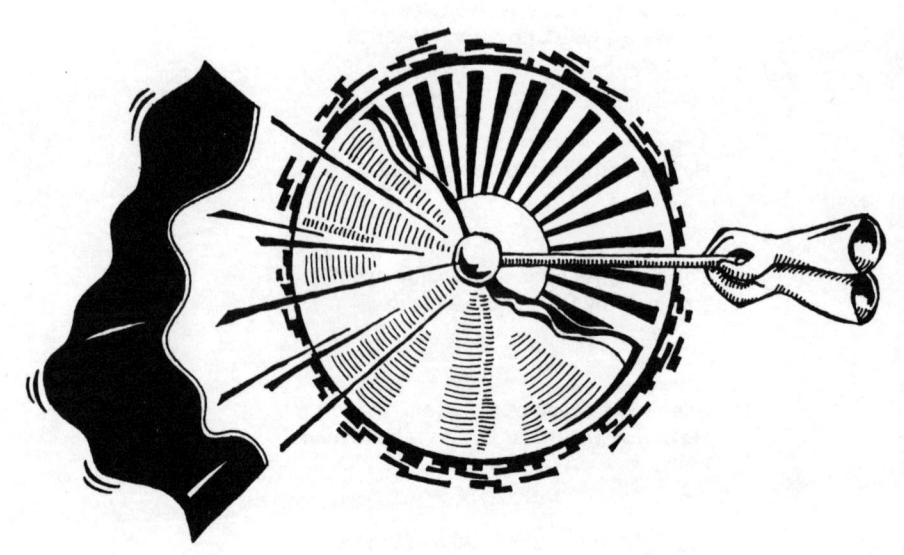

DARKNESS IS GONE

Darkness is gone, daylight has come.
The Son of God and man arises with the dawn.
Death loses its sinister sting,
God's promise to do a new thing
Is done,. and Hallelujah
Earth joins heaven to sing.

2. See now the cross, see now the grave.
They vacant celebrate how God's foolishness can save.
The reject nailed up as a fraud
Is raised by the power of God
And lives, so, Hallelujah.
Scatter the news abroad.

Greener the grass, brighter the sun;
The God-loved world proclaims a new age has begun.
Creation is decked for her guest
Who, freed from his grave clothes is dressed
In light and, Hallelujah,
Tells that the earth is blessed.

4. The needed trust, the longed-for peace
Are passed as hands from sword and shackle are released.
The violence of hate reigns no more.
The victory of love is the core
Of hope and, Hallelujah,
Love means an open door.

'The Kingdom comes' the King proclaims:
Justice and joy abound where Christ-filled faith pertains.
Religion, remote and typecast
Is gone and the future is vast.
New tongues sing 'Hallelujah,
God is for us at last.'

6. Enrol the drum, enlist the gong
To celebrate in sound that right has conquered wrong.
Join hands with the neighbour unknown,
Unite through the love that is shown
In Christ, for, Hallelujah,
He is our Lord alone.

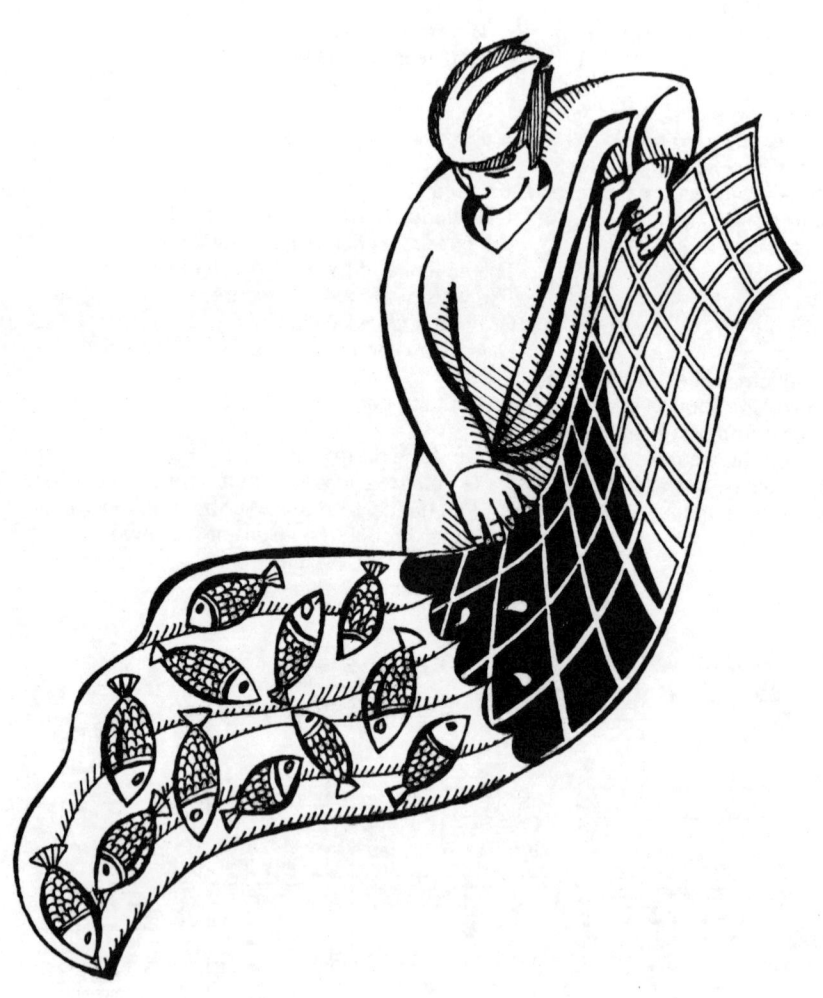

1. 'James and Andrew, Peter and John,
   Men of temper, talent and tide,
   Your nets are empty, empty and bare,
   Cast them now on the opposite side.'

2. 'Jesus, you're only a carpenter's son:
   Joints and joists are part of your trade.
   But ours the skill to harvest the deep.
   Why presume to come to our aid?'

3. 'Friends of mine and brothers through love,
   I mean more than fishing for food.
   I call your skill to service my will,
   Call your lives to harvest the good.'

4. 'Cast your nets where you think is right,
   Spend your lives where you think is need.
   But if you long for that which is best,
   Let it be on my word you feed.'

5. 'Stir then the waters, Lord, stir up the wind.
   Stir the hope that needs to be stretched.
   Stir up the love that needs to be ground,
   Stir the faith that needs to be fetched.'

6. James and Andrew, Peter and John
   And the girls who walked by his side.
   Hear how the Lord calls each by their name
   Asking all to turn like the tide.

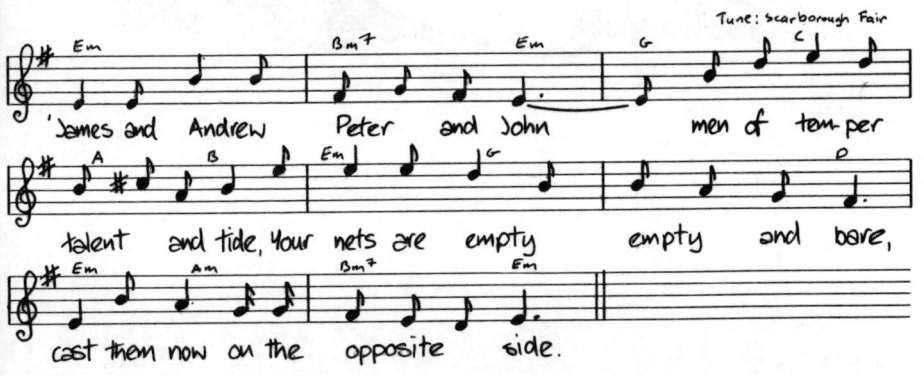

1. From heaven to here and from here to heaven
   Is a distance less than tissue thin.
   And it's trod by him who in the stranger's guise
   Is made known when once he's welcomed in.

   Chorus: So, come Lord Christ in the stranger's guise
   Known both through Scriptures and through broken bread.
   Your kingdom come and on earth let Your will be done
   For Your people are here to be led.

2. The road he travels is the road to life
   Though it passes through death and hell.
   But each step that's taken is with confidence
   For he knows with God all will be well.

3. The folk who journey on the road with Christ
   Are the ones who've left their selves behind.
   Their song is taught them by the deaf and dumb
   Their horizon is shown by the blind.

4. The love that's shared along the royal road
   Is a love not found standing still
   It lives and grows wherever faith is known
   As a movement grounded in God's will.

5. From heaven to here and from here to heaven
   Is a distance less than tissue thin.
   And it's trod by those who meet the risen Christ
   As a stranger to be welcomed in.

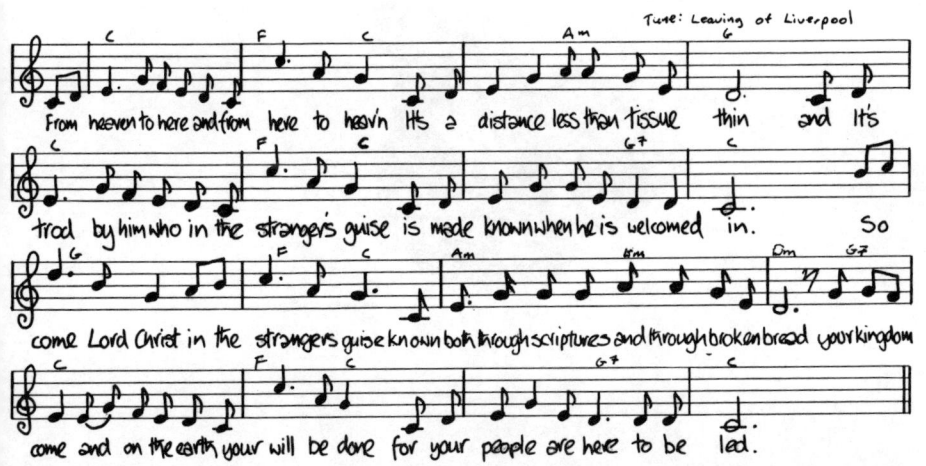

LO, I AM WITH YOU

1. Lo, I am with you to the end of the world.
   Lo, I am with you to the end of the world.
   Lo, I am with you; Lo, I am with you;
   Lo, I am with you to the end of the world.

2. Lo, I am with you when you leave self behind . . .

3. Lo, I am with you in the struggle for peace . . .

4. Lo, I am with you when you suffer for love . . .

5. Lo, I am with you in the way of the cross . . .

6. Lo, I am with you in the darkness of death . . .

7. Lo, I am with you to the end of the world.

SONGS OF THE INCARNATION
Bell & Maule